Happiness: An Analysis of a Desire

Iraya Ahemón García

Published by Ediciones Doble A, 2024.

While every precaution has been taken in the preparation of this book, the publisher assumes no responsibility for errors or omissions, or for damages resulting from the use of the information contained herein.

HAPPINESS: AN ANALYSIS OF A DESIRE

First edition. November 19, 2024.

Copyright © 2024 Iraya Ahemón García.

ISBN: 979-8230723103

Written by Iraya Ahemón García.

Table of Contents

Introduction 1
Chapter 1: What Is Happiness? 7
Chapter 2: The Psychology of Happiness 19
Chapter 3: The Benefits of Happiness.................................. 27
Chapter 4: What Prevents Us From Being Happy? 35
Chapter 5: Strategies to Cultivate Happiness.................... 45
Chapter 6: Relationships and Happiness 57
Chapter 7: Happiness at Work 67
Chapter 8: Happiness in the Digital Age 73
Chapter 9: Happiness and Health 79
Chapter 10: The Search for Meaning................................... 85
Chapter 11: Happiness in Different Cultures 89
Chapter 12: Conclusions 95

Introduction

Happiness is one of the most universal and sought-after emotions among people worldwide. Beyond cultural, historical, or personal differences, we all aspire to experience it and, even more, to sustain it over time. Essentially, happiness can be understood as a positive emotional state accompanied by a sense of well-being, life satisfaction, and personal fulfillment. Although its specific definition varies from person to person, there are common elements often associated with it, such as joy, a sense of purpose, and emotional balance that allows us to face daily challenges with resilience.

Throughout history, the pursuit of happiness has been a central topic for philosophers, poets, scientists, and thinkers across various disciplines. For Aristotle, for instance, happiness was the ultimate goal of human life, the supreme objective toward which all actions should be directed. According to him, this state was achieved through the practice of virtues such as justice, friendship, and wisdom, in a balance between pleasure and reason. Conversely, Epicurus argued that happiness lay in the pursuit of simple pleasures, the absence of pain, and mental tranquility, while Plato linked this state to knowledge and the harmony between the soul and the world.

Today, happiness continues to be a subject of study and reflection, but with a more scientific and multidisciplinary approach. Positive psychology, a field that has gained significant relevance in recent decades, has focused on investigating the factors that contribute to emotional well-being and life satisfaction. Studies in this area have identified key elements such as social relationships, gratitude, optimism, the ability to manage stress, and emotional resilience. Moreover, it has been shown that happiness is not merely a passive state but can be cultivated through conscious practices and habits.

Various theories have sought to explain how to achieve and maintain happiness. The flow theory, proposed by Mihály Csíkszentmihályi, suggests that people reach their highest level of happiness when they are completely immersed in activities that are meaningful and challenging. This state, known as "flow," involves total concentration, a loss of awareness of time, and a sense of mastery and accomplishment. On the other hand, self-determination theory posits that happiness arises from fulfilling three basic needs: autonomy, competence, and social connection.

Beyond psychology, other disciplines have also studied happiness from different perspectives. In the field of economics, Bhutan's Gross National Happiness Index has been a pioneering model that prioritizes citizens' well-being over traditional economic growth. This approach has inspired global debates on how to measure a society's progress, placing values such as health, education, and sustainability at the forefront. In public health, research has shown that happiness has a direct impact on physical and mental health, reducing the risk of cardiovascular diseases, strengthening the immune system, and increasing longevity.

Ultimately, happiness is a complex phenomenon that cannot be reduced to a single formula or a universal approach. It is a dynamic state that depends on both internal factors, such as emotions and beliefs, and external factors, such as social and cultural circumstances. Despite its complexity, efforts to understand and cultivate happiness share a common goal: to improve quality of life and promote holistic well-being for individuals and communities.

With each new advance in the understanding of happiness, we move a little closer to integrating this valuable state into our lives, not as a distant goal but as an everyday experience that allows us to live with greater fulfillment and meaning.

A Brief Overview of Happiness Throughout History

The study of happiness has been a central theme in the history of human thought, addressed from various philosophical, psychological, sociological, and scientific perspectives. Below is an expanded and enriched review of the main approaches and authors who have explored this concept over time:

1. Ancient Philosophy

Happiness was a recurring topic in Greek philosophy, regarded as the ultimate goal of human life. Aristotle, in his work *Nicomachean Ethics*, defined happiness (*eudaimonia*) as the full realization of human virtues. For him, practicing virtues such as justice, friendship, and wisdom led to a balanced and happy life. Epicurus, on the other hand, proposed a more hedonistic view: happiness lay in the pursuit of pleasure, understood as the absence of physical pain and emotional disturbance. Socrates and Plato also reflected on happiness, linking it to wisdom and the knowledge of good within the framework of a virtuous and just life.

2. Modern Philosophy

With the advent of modernity, the reflection on happiness was enriched by new perspectives. René Descartes, in his *Discourse on the Method*, proposed that happiness was related to reason and contemplation, resulting from an orderly life guided by logical thought. In the 18th century, Immanuel Kant argued that happiness was not an end in itself but a consequence of acting in accordance with morality and duty. Jean-Jacques Rousseau, in *Emile, or On Education*, linked happiness to a life in harmony with nature and to an education that fostered virtue and individual freedom.

3. Psychology

Psychology began to take an interest in the study of happiness in the 20th century, reaching its peak with the emergence of positive psychology in the 1990s. Abraham Maslow, with his theory of the hierarchy of needs, highlighted self-actualization as one of the keys to achieving happiness. Martin Seligman, one of the founders of positive psychology, proposed the theory of well-being based on five pillars: positive emotions, engagement, social relationships, a sense of purpose, and accomplishments. This approach demonstrated that happiness is not a passive state but an active experience that can be cultivated through specific habits and practices.

4. Sociology

Sociology has addressed the study of happiness by analyzing how social, cultural, religious, and economic factors influence it. Émile Durkheim, one of the pioneers in this discipline, asserted that happiness was closely tied to the degree of social integration and participation in collective activities. Contemporary sociologists have explored topics such as the impact of social inequalities, family dynamics, and globalization on people's emotional well-being.

5. Neuroscience

In recent decades, neuroscience has revolutionized the understanding of happiness by exploring the brain processes involved. It has been discovered that regions such as the prefrontal cortex, the limbic system, and the nucleus accumbens play a key role in generating positive emotions and sensations of pleasure. Research has shown that practices such as meditation and mindfulness can increase activity in these areas, promoting a greater sense of well-being.

6. Economics

The economics of well-being has introduced tools to measure happiness on a societal level and evaluate its relationship with economic development. Bhutan's Gross National Happiness Index has been an inspiring example, prioritizing citizens' well-being over traditional economic growth. Richard Layard, a British economist, has advocated for public policies that promote happiness, demonstrating that emotional well-being has a direct impact on productivity and social cohesion.

7. Public Health

In the field of public health, it has been shown that happiness not only improves quality of life but also has significant effects on physical and mental health. Happier people tend to have stronger immune systems, lower risks of chronic diseases, and greater life expectancy. Promoting emotional well-being has become a key strategy for preventing diseases and fostering healthy lifestyles.

IRAYA AHEMÓN GARCÍA

Key Works on Happiness

Throughout history, various authors have captured their reflections on happiness in works that remain relevant today. Some of the most notable are:

- *Nicomachean Ethics* by Aristotle: A fundamental treatise on happiness and virtues.
- *Confessions* by Saint Augustine: Reflections on happiness from a spiritual perspective.
- *Discourse on the Method* by René Descartes: A rationalist approach to the pursuit of happiness.
- *Emile, or On Education* by Jean-Jacques Rousseau: A work linking education and happiness.
- *Walden* by Henry David Thoreau: A defense of simplicity and connection with nature as sources of happiness.
- *The Conquest of Happiness* by Bertrand Russell: A philosophical analysis of the causes of unhappiness and how to overcome them.
- *The Art of Happiness* by the Dalai Lama and Howard Cutler: A practical and spiritual perspective on achieving happiness.
- *The Paradox of Choice* by Barry Schwartz: An analysis of how decision-making impacts our happiness.
- *Authentic Happiness* by Martin Seligman: A scientific and practical approach to cultivating well-being.

Chapter 1: What Is Happiness?

Happiness is a positive emotional state characterized by feelings of pleasure, joy, and satisfaction in life. It is a subjective and personal experience that can be influenced by both internal and external factors, such as interpersonal relationships, success at work, physical and mental health, among others.

Happiness is a topic widely studied in psychology, and it has been shown to have positive effects on mental and physical health. People who are happier tend to have a higher quality of life, better interpersonal relationships, greater resilience, and better capacity to handle stress.

However, it is important to remember that happiness is not a permanent and constant state in life. We all experience emotional ups and downs, and it is normal to have days when we do not feel happy. Furthermore, happiness is not the only goal in life, and it is important to find a balance between the pursuit of happiness and the acceptance of life's challenges and difficulties.

Definitions of Happiness

Happiness is a broad and complex concept that has been debated for centuries across different disciplines and cultures. Although there is no single and universally accepted definition of happiness, it can be understood as a positive and lasting emotional state that involves a sense of well-being and satisfaction with life.

From a psychological perspective, happiness has been studied as a combination of three main components: the emotional component, which includes feelings of pleasure, joy, and satisfaction; the cognitive component, which refers to the subjective evaluation of life and the perception of progress toward important goals; and the behavioral component, which involves participation in meaningful and rewarding activities.

In terms of philosophy, happiness has been approached in different ways. From the perspective of hedonism, happiness is understood as the pursuit of pleasure and the avoidance of pain. For Stoicism, happiness is achieved through virtue and the acceptance of life's circumstances. And from the perspective of utilitarianism, happiness is measured in terms of the amount of well-being generated for the majority of people.

From a sociological perspective, happiness has been studied as a social phenomenon influenced by factors such as culture, religion, economy, and politics. For example, some studies have found that people in countries with higher levels of economic equality and democracy are more likely to be happy.

Happiness has also been linked to other concepts such as mental health, well-being, resilience, and quality of life. For instance, the World Health Organization defines mental health as "a state of well-being in which the individual realizes his or her own abilities, can cope with the normal stresses of life, can work productively and fruitfully, and is able to contribute to his or her community." In this sense, happiness can be considered a key component of mental health.

In research on happiness, some factors have been identified that appear to be associated with higher levels of happiness. These include having meaningful and supportive social relationships, having a purpose and sense of life, regularly experiencing positive emotions, being engaged in meaningful and rewarding activities, and having a sense of control over one's life.

Ultimately, happiness is a subjective concept that is experienced and understood differently by each person. Happiness can be a goal for some, while for others, it may be a state of mind that arises spontaneously. What is clear is that happiness is a fundamental aspect of human life, and that the pursuit and cultivation of happiness can have significant benefits for well-being and quality of life.

Common Definitions of Happiness

Happiness is a subjective and multifaceted concept that can have different definitions depending on each individual's perspective. Below are some common definitions of happiness:

1. **Positive emotional state:** Happiness can be defined as a positive emotional state characterized by a sense of well-being, satisfaction, and joy.
2. **Absence of suffering:** Some people define happiness as the absence of suffering or emotional pain, meaning the ability to live a life free from stress, anxiety, and worries.
3. **Achievement of goals and objectives:** Happiness can also be related to the ability to achieve personal goals and objectives, which provides a sense of accomplishment and satisfaction.
4. **Psychological and physical well-being:** Happiness can be related to an overall state of well-being, which

includes both physical and mental health. People may feel happy when they feel healthy and fit.
5. **Interpersonal and social connection:** Happiness may also be related to social relationships and interpersonal connection. People may feel happy when they have close friends and family with whom they can share their lives.

Differences Between Happiness and Other Positive Emotional States

Happiness is one of the most well-known and desirable positive emotional states, but there are other emotional states that are also positive and distinct from happiness. This text explores some of the differences between happiness and other positive emotional states.

Happiness is an emotional state of general well-being characterized by feelings of joy, satisfaction, and pleasure. It is a lasting emotional state that is related to a fulfilling and satisfying life. In contrast, joy is an intense and temporary emotional state experienced when achieving something or having a positive experience. Joy is usually related to a specific event, while happiness is a more generalized state.

Gratitude is another positive emotional state related to happiness, but it is different. Gratitude is a feeling of appreciation for what one has in life, and it involves valuing the good things in one's life. Gratitude can be a temporary emotional state, but it can also be an attitude or a way of life that is maintained over time.

HAPPINESS: AN ANALYSIS OF A DESIRE

Love is another positive emotional state that differs from happiness. Love is characterized by a sense of deep connection and affection toward another person. Love can be a lasting feeling that endures over time and can be a source of happiness, but it is not the same as happiness. Happiness is a generalized emotional state, while love is an emotional state directed toward a person or a group of people.

Peace is another positive emotional state that is related to happiness but is distinct. Peace is characterized by a feeling of inner calm and harmony. It is an emotional state associated with the absence of stress, conflict, and worry. Peace can be a temporary state, but it can also be an attitude or a way of life that is consistently maintained.

Hope is another positive emotional state that differs from happiness. Hope is characterized by a feeling of confidence and optimism about the future. It is an emotional state associated with the belief in the possibility of achieving goals and realizing dreams. Hope can be a temporary state, but it can also be an attitude or a way of life that is consistently maintained.

In summary, happiness is a generalized emotional state associated with a sense of well-being and fulfillment in life. Other positive emotional states, such as joy, gratitude, love, peace, and hope, can be distinct from happiness in terms of their duration, intensity, and focus. All these emotional states can be valuable and beneficial for a person's emotional and mental well-being and can be cultivated and maintained in different ways.

IRAYA AHEMÓN GARCÍA

The Value of Happiness in Human Life

Happiness is a topic that has been the subject of study and reflection by philosophers, psychologists, and social scientists throughout history. Although there is no universally accepted definition of happiness, it can be understood as a positive and lasting emotional state in which a person feels satisfied with their life and experiences a sense of well-being.

The value of happiness in human life is immeasurable. Numerous studies have shown that happier people tend to have better interpersonal relationships, higher self-esteem, greater resilience, and better performance in various areas of their lives. Additionally, happiness can have a positive impact on people's physical and mental health, reducing stress and improving sleep quality.

One of the most remarkable aspects of happiness is its multifaceted nature. Happiness does not depend solely on external factors, such as wealth or social status, but is also influenced by internal factors, such as personality and how a person perceives and processes information. Happiness can also be influenced by biological factors, such as genes and brain chemistry.

Another important aspect of happiness is that it is not a permanent state. Happiness can fluctuate over time, and people may experience different levels of happiness depending on their life circumstances and personal evolution. For this reason, it is important not to view happiness as a final goal but as a process in which a person continuously works to maintain a state of emotional well-being.

HAPPINESS: AN ANALYSIS OF A DESIRE

Despite the numerous studies conducted on happiness, much about this topic remains unknown. Some researchers suggest that happiness is largely a matter of perspective and that people can learn to be happier by changing their way of thinking and perceiving the world around them. Other researchers focus on the role of biological and genetic factors in happiness.

In any case, it is important to recognize that happiness is not a state that can be achieved simply through the pursuit of pleasure or the satisfaction of material desires. True and lasting happiness is based on the satisfaction and meaning that a person finds in their life and in the relationships they establish with others.

In conclusion, the value of happiness in human life is immeasurable. Happiness can have a positive impact on various aspects of a person's life, including their interpersonal relationships, self-esteem, and physical and mental health. Happiness is a complex and multifaceted emotional state that is influenced by internal and external factors and can fluctuate over time. It is important not to view happiness as a final goal but as a continuous process of emotional well-being that requires constant effort and attention.

Why Do We Place So Much Importance on Happiness?

The importance of happiness lies in the fact that it is an emotional state we all wish to experience. Happiness is a positive emotion that makes us feel good, motivated, and gives us a general sense of well-being in our lives. The pursuit of happiness has become a goal for many people, often associated with life satisfaction and personal success.

Happiness has several benefits for our physical and mental health. Scientific evidence suggests that people who frequently experience positive emotions have a lower risk of developing chronic diseases, such as heart disease, diabetes, and cancer. Moreover, happiness can help us better manage stress and anxiety, improving our emotional and psychological state.

Additionally, happiness can enhance our interpersonal relationships and our ability to interact socially. Happy people tend to be friendlier, have a more positive attitude, and are more likely to help others. Furthermore, happiness can also improve our work and academic performance, as it makes us feel more motivated and better equipped to face challenges.

On the other hand, some authors argue that the importance placed on happiness in today's society can create excessive pressure to achieve it, which in turn can negatively affect our emotional well-being. In his book *The Imperative of Happiness*, philosopher Eduardo Infante suggests that the obsessive pursuit of happiness can lead to constant dissatisfaction, as we strive to attain an emotional state that is fleeting and difficult to sustain over time.

The importance placed on happiness is due to the multiple benefits it can provide to our physical and mental health, as well as our ability to interact socially and perform in various areas of life. However, it is important to keep in mind that the pursuit of happiness should not become an obsession, as this can negatively affect our emotional well-being.

HAPPINESS: AN ANALYSIS OF A DESIRE

Why Is It So Hard to Be Happy?

Being happy can be difficult because many aspects of life can interfere with our happiness. Sometimes, we may feel trapped by stress, anxiety, sadness, loneliness, or a lack of purpose. Additionally, our culture and society may impose unrealistic ideals of happiness and success, making us feel as though we never measure up to these expectations.

There are also biological and genetic factors that influence our happiness. Some people have a natural predisposition to be happier or less happy than others, and brain chemistry and hormonal factors can also affect our mood.

However, while it may be challenging, it is not impossible to be happy. There are many things we can do to increase our happiness, such as cultivating positive relationships, practicing gratitude, finding meaning and purpose in our lives, taking care of our physical and mental health, and finding ways to manage stress and anxiety. With some effort and dedication, we can learn to be happier and find satisfaction in our lives.

There are several biological and genetic factors that can influence our happiness. One of them is the brain's reward system, which is associated with the release of dopamine, a neurotransmitter related to pleasure and motivation. People with a more sensitive reward system may experience more pleasure and happiness in response to positive situations, while those with a less sensitive system may find it harder to feel happy.

Additionally, certain genes have been identified as being related to happiness. For example, there is a gene called *5-HTT*, which is associated with serotonin regulation, another neurotransmitter linked to mood. Some people have a variant of this gene that appears to be related to a higher susceptibility to depression and anxiety.

Hormonal factors also play a role in our happiness. Oxytocin, for instance, is a hormone released in the brain when we form close and affectionate connections with others. This hormone can help reduce anxiety and stress and promote feelings of happiness and well-being.

Can We Live Without Being Happy?

Yes, it is possible to live without being happy. Happiness is a complex and multifaceted emotion that can be difficult to define and achieve in everyday life. Many people experience periods of sadness, anxiety, or dissatisfaction at some point in their lives and still manage to move forward.

Moreover, life is a mix of highs and lows, and not all moments can be happy. Often, people face challenges and obstacles that may leave them feeling overwhelmed or unmotivated. However, these experiences can also serve as opportunities for personal growth and the development of resilience.

It is important to note that happiness is not the only goal in life. Many people find meaning and purpose in their relationships, work, hobbies, community, and other areas. Often, individuals feel more satisfied and fulfilled when they pursue meaningful goals and contribute to something greater than themselves.

Here are some key aspects that can influence a person's ability to live without being happy:

HAPPINESS: AN ANALYSIS OF A DESIRE

1. **Resilience:** Resilience refers to a person's ability to quickly recover from difficult or adverse situations. People with high resilience are better able to handle life's challenges and adapt to them. If someone is not happy but has strong resilience, they may still lead a satisfying and productive life.
2. **Purpose and Meaning in Life:** Having a purpose and a sense of meaning can be very important for some people. If someone has a clear and meaningful goal in life, they may feel satisfied and motivated even if they are not happy all the time.
3. **Social Support:** Social support is crucial for emotional well-being. If a person has friends and family who support and care for them, they may feel less lonely and more capable of dealing with life's challenges, even if they are not consistently happy.
4. **Mental Health:** If a person is not happy and is also dealing with mental health issues, it can be challenging to lead a satisfying life. Depression, anxiety, and other disorders can make someone feel overwhelmed and hopeless. Seeking treatment and support for these issues can be essential to improving quality of life.

Chapter 2: The Psychology of Happiness

Happiness is an emotional state desired by most people, and its pursuit has been a recurring theme throughout human history. The psychology of happiness is a discipline focused on understanding the factors that influence happiness and emotional well-being. This field has gained significant relevance today, as its study can help improve people's quality of life and prevent emotional disorders.

The psychology of happiness has evolved over time and has been influenced by various theoretical approaches. One of the main figures in this discipline is Martin Seligman, who proposed the theory of well-being and positive psychology. According to this theory, emotional well-being can be achieved through the presence of positive emotions, engagement in meaningful activities, and a sense of purpose and meaning in life. This theory has been widely accepted and has had a significant influence on the psychology of happiness.

Another important figure in the psychology of happiness is Ed Diener, who has studied happiness and subjective well-being throughout his career. Diener has developed various measures to assess happiness and subjective well-being and has demonstrated the importance of these factors for people's health and well-being.

The psychology of happiness has shown that happiness is not only related to the absence of negative emotions but also to the presence of positive emotions. Furthermore, it has been found that happiness is associated with better academic and work performance, greater resilience to stress, and improved physical and mental health.

The psychology of happiness has also demonstrated that happiness is a dynamic emotional state that can be influenced by various factors. Some factors found to affect happiness include personality, interpersonal relationships, physical activity, meditation, and gratitude.

In conclusion, the psychology of happiness is a discipline focused on understanding the factors that influence people's happiness and emotional well-being. This field has evolved over time and has been shaped by different theoretical approaches. The psychology of happiness has highlighted the importance of positive emotions, engagement in meaningful activities, and a sense of purpose and meaning in life in the pursuit of happiness. Moreover, it has been found that happiness is linked to better academic and work performance, greater resilience to stress, and improved physical and mental health.

How Our Brain Works in Relation to Happiness

Happiness is a complex and multifaceted emotional state that involves both cognitive and physiological aspects. The brain is the central organ responsible for processing and regulating emotions, playing a fundamental role in the experience of happiness.

In general terms, happiness is associated with the activation of various areas of the brain, including the nucleus accumbens, the ventromedial prefrontal cortex, and the amygdala. These brain regions are involved in the regulation of dopamine, a

HAPPINESS: AN ANALYSIS OF A DESIRE

neurotransmitter associated with feelings of pleasure and reward.

The nucleus accumbens is a brain region that becomes active when we experience pleasure and reward, whether from obtaining something desired or engaging in enjoyable activities. This region is involved in the release of dopamine, which enhances feelings of well-being and satisfaction.

The ventromedial prefrontal cortex, on the other hand, is a brain region associated with decision-making and emotional regulation. Studies have shown that this area is more active in people who report high levels of happiness, suggesting that the ability to regulate positive and negative emotions is linked to happiness.

Finally, the amygdala is a brain region associated with emotional responses to fear and anxiety, as well as to positive stimuli. Research has found that people with higher levels of happiness have a more active amygdala in response to positive stimuli, indicating that this brain region also plays a role in the experience of happiness.

The brain and happiness are closely interconnected, and understanding this relationship can provide valuable insights into how to improve emotional well-being. Overall, the brain is responsible for regulating mood and emotions, and several brain structures and processes are involved in generating happiness.

One of the most important brain structures related to happiness is the reward system. This system comprises several structures, including the nucleus accumbens, the ventral tegmental area, and the medial prefrontal cortex. These structures work together to release dopamine, a neurotransmitter associated with feelings of reward and pleasure. When we receive a reward or experience something enjoyable, the reward system activates and releases dopamine, making us feel happy.

Another critical structure related to happiness is the hippocampus, located in the medial temporal lobe of the brain. The hippocampus plays a key role in memory consolidation and emotion, and it has been found to be involved in encoding happy memories. When we experience something happy, the hippocampus records this experience and stores it in long-term memory, allowing us to recall and relive the happy experience in the future.

In addition to the reward system and the hippocampus, other brain structures and processes are involved in happiness. For example, the anterior cingulate cortex, located in the frontal lobe, is involved in processing emotion and decision-making. This area has been found to activate during positive emotions such as happiness and joy.

The amygdala, located in the temporal lobe, also plays a role in happiness. It is involved in evaluating and processing emotional information and has been found to be more active in people who report higher levels of happiness.

It is important to note that happiness is a complex concept that can be challenging to define and measure. There are many theories about what makes people happy, and research in this area is constantly evolving. Some factors associated with happiness include social relationships, job satisfaction, physical and mental health, and religiosity or spirituality.

In summary, the brain is intrinsically linked to happiness, and several brain structures and processes are involved in generating positive emotions. Although happiness is a complex and multifaceted concept, research in this area can provide valuable insights into how to improve emotional well-being.

The Components of Happiness

Happiness is a complex and multifaceted emotional state that can be influenced by a wide range of internal and external factors. While the components of happiness may vary from person to person, some common factors contributing to happiness include:

1. **Healthy relationships:** Positive social connections, such as family and friendships, can be a fundamental component of happiness.
2. **Purpose and meaning:** Having a sense of purpose in life and feeling that our actions positively impact the world can enhance happiness.
3. **Achievement and success:** Accomplishing goals and succeeding in our activities can provide a sense of satisfaction and happiness.
4. **Health and well-being:** Taking care of our physical and mental health, including regular physical activity and a healthy diet, can contribute to happiness.
5. **Gratitude and appreciation:** The ability to appreciate the good things in life and feel grateful for them can increase happiness.
6. **Pleasure and enjoyment:** Experiencing pleasure and enjoyment in our daily activities can also be an important component of happiness.

It is important to note that these components are not exhaustive, and happiness is a subjective experience influenced by a variety of individual factors.

The components of happiness can be categorized into three main areas: emotions, cognitions, and behaviors. These are described in more detail below:

Emotions

Positive emotions, such as joy, gratitude, and love, are essential for happiness. When we experience positive emotions, the brain's reward system is activated, releasing chemicals such as dopamine that make us feel good. Moreover, positive emotions help us develop resilience and better cope with challenges and difficult situations. On the other hand, it is also important to learn how to manage negative emotions, such as sadness or stress, to improve our emotional well-being.

Cognitions

The beliefs and thoughts we have about ourselves and our surroundings also influence our happiness. Positive self-esteem, acceptance of reality, and the ability to find meaning in experiences are some of the cognitive components that contribute to happiness. Self-esteem relates to how we value ourselves, while acceptance of reality refers to the ability to adapt to life's circumstances, including challenges and losses. Finding meaning in experiences can help us make sense of our lives and find purpose.

Behaviors

Our daily actions also influence our happiness. Adopting healthy habits, such as regular exercise, sufficient sleep, and a balanced diet, can significantly improve mental and emotional health. Similarly, nurturing social relationships and dedicating time to activities we enjoy can enhance our well-being. It is important to recognize that the behaviors that bring happiness vary from person to person, so identifying which habits and activities work best for each individual is crucial.

Psychological Theories of Happiness

Happiness has been a topic of interest in psychology for decades, and numerous theories have emerged to explain how happiness can be achieved and what factors influence it. Below are some of the most notable psychological theories of happiness:

Maslow's Hierarchy of Needs

Abraham Maslow proposed in his theory of the hierarchy of needs that individuals have a series of needs that must be fulfilled to achieve happiness. These needs range from basic necessities like food, shelter, and safety to higher needs such as self-esteem and self-actualization.

Maslow argued that once basic needs are met, individuals can focus on fulfilling higher-level needs, which allow them to achieve a sense of happiness and well-being.

Hedonic Adaptation Theory

The hedonic adaptation theory suggests that people have a stable level of happiness to which they tend to return after experiencing both positive and negative events. According to this theory, individuals adapt to changes in their circumstances and life events, whether good or bad, and eventually revert to their baseline level of happiness.

This theory implies that the constant pursuit of happiness through external positive events may be futile, as individuals eventually adapt to these changes. Instead, it emphasizes finding happiness through internal processes and well-being practices.

Self-Determination Theory

The self-determination theory posits that individuals have three basic psychological needs: the need for autonomy, the need for competence, and the need for relatedness with others. Fulfilling these needs can lead to a sense of happiness and well-being.

- **Autonomy** refers to the sense of having control and choice in life.
- **Competence** refers to the feeling of being capable of achieving goals and challenging oneself.
- **Relatedness** refers to the feeling of belonging and being close to others.

Chapter 3: The Benefits of Happiness

Happiness has been a topic of interest in psychology and scientific research for decades. Although happiness is a subjective concept that can be difficult to define and measure, there is a consensus that happiness is a key component of psychological well-being.

Happiness is not only a pleasant emotional state but has also been shown to have multiple benefits for health and well-being. People who experience higher levels of happiness often enjoy better social relationships, greater resilience to stress, and improved physical and mental health.

Research has demonstrated that happiness can also have a positive effect on workplace and academic success, as well as decision-making. Happier individuals tend to be more productive and creative and are also more likely to make informed and effective decisions.

Moreover, happiness has been linked to a longer and healthier life. A 2011 study found that happier people were 35% less likely to die during the five-year follow-up period compared to less happy individuals. Other studies have found that happiness can improve immune function and reduce the risk of chronic diseases such as cardiovascular disease.

Happiness is more than just feeling good; it has multiple benefits for physical and mental health as well as success in life. As such, understanding how to cultivate happiness and make it an integral part of our lives is essential.

IRAYA AHEMÓN GARCÍA

Happiness as a Predictor of a Healthy and Successful Life

Happiness has been studied extensively in psychology and scientific research for decades. Although happiness is a subjective concept that can be challenging to define and measure, evidence suggests that happiness is an important predictor of a healthy and successful life.

Happiness and health are closely related. A large body of research demonstrates that happier people have better health outcomes compared to less happy individuals. Studies have shown that happy people are less likely to develop chronic diseases such as cardiovascular disease, diabetes, hypertension, and mental health issues like depression and anxiety (Lyubomirsky, 2008).

A longitudinal study conducted by Lyubomirsky and colleagues (2011) found that happier individuals were 35% less likely to die during the five-year follow-up period compared to less happy individuals. Another study revealed that people who frequently experienced positive emotions had a significantly lower risk of developing cardiovascular disease (Pressman et al., 2013).

Happiness is also linked to a better quality of life. Happier people report greater life satisfaction, better interpersonal relationships, and a stronger sense of purpose in life (Diener, Lucas, and Oishi, 2018).

For instance, a 2012 study found that individuals who reported feeling happier also had a higher quality of life in terms of emotional well-being, interpersonal relationships, and a sense of purpose in life (Huppert, Baylis, and Keverne, 2012).

Additionally, happiness has been linked to greater job satisfaction, which can contribute to career success (Lyubomirsky, King, and Diener, 2005).

Happiness can also predict life success in terms of academic and professional achievements. A 2016 study found that happier college students were more likely to perform well academically and secure employment after graduation (Mak et al., 2016). Furthermore, happiness has been associated with higher workplace achievement and greater productivity (Lyubomirsky, King, and Diener, 2005).

Happiness has also been linked to greater resilience to stress. Happier individuals appear to be better at managing stress and recovering more quickly from stressful events (Lyubomirsky, King, and Diener, 2005). Additionally, happiness may have a buffering effect on the negative impacts of stress on physical and mental health (Cohen, Pressman, and Black, 2016).

Happiness is also associated with a longer and healthier life. A 2011 study found that happier people were 35% less likely to die during the five-year follow-up period compared to less happy individuals (Chida and Steptoe, 2008). Furthermore, happiness has been linked to better immune function and a reduced risk of chronic illnesses such as cardiovascular disease

Happiness as a Promoter of Satisfying Interpersonal Relationships

Satisfying interpersonal relationships are those based on respect, trust, communication, and mutual support. These relationships allow us to share our emotions, needs, interests, and values with others who accept and value us. They also help us develop social skills, resolve conflicts constructively, and face life's challenges.

The importance of satisfying interpersonal relationships in happiness lies in the sense of belonging, security, and well-being they provide. Scientific studies have shown that people with fulfilling interpersonal relationships are happier, healthier, and live longer than those without them. Moreover, these relationships enable us to express and receive affection, gratitude, recognition, and emotional support, which boosts our self-esteem and life satisfaction.

Thus, cultivating and maintaining satisfying interpersonal relationships is one of the keys to achieving happiness. To do so, it is important to dedicate time and attention to the people who matter to us, show interest in their lives, listen to them empathetically, respect their opinions and feelings, offer help when needed, and celebrate their achievements. In this way, we can build strong and lasting bonds that make us feel happier.

Happiness plays a crucial role in interpersonal relationships, as happy people tend to be more sociable, kind, and empathetic, facilitating the creation of satisfying and long-lasting relationships.

When people feel happy, they have more energy and enthusiasm to interact with others, which can increase their self-confidence and ability to connect. Additionally, happiness can improve a person's mood, making them more attractive and enjoyable to be around.

Happiness also positively impacts how people handle conflicts and difficult situations in relationships. Happy individuals tend to be more respectful and understanding, which helps reduce tension and disagreements.

Happiness can be a key factor in satisfying interpersonal relationships, as happy people often have a more positive and optimistic outlook on life. This positive attitude influences how they interact with others, making them more appealing and fostering social connections.

Furthermore, happy individuals are often more empathetic and compassionate, making them more likely to help others and offer support in difficult times. This capacity for empathy and support is essential for building fulfilling interpersonal relationships, as it fosters trust, respect, and closeness.

Happiness also influences how people manage conflicts and challenging situations in relationships. Happy people tend to be more flexible and resilient, allowing them to adapt better to changes and overcome difficulties. Additionally, happiness can improve a person's mood, making it easier to handle and resolve conflicts.

Happiness as a Promoter of Resilience and Positive Stress Coping

Happiness is an emotional state characterized by positive sensations and elevated emotions such as satisfaction, fulfillment, and well-being in daily life. This emotional state is closely linked to resilience and positive stress coping.

Resilience refers to the ability to face and adapt to adverse situations. It involves recovering from and emerging stronger after difficult circumstances.

IRAYA AHEMÓN GARCÍA

Happy individuals often demonstrate greater capacity to face challenges and overcome stress. People with a positive outlook on life and who experience positive emotions are better equipped to adapt and handle situations effectively.

Studies have also shown that happiness correlates with emotional intelligence, which is linked to better stress management. People with higher emotional intelligence can identify, manage, and use their emotions to navigate difficult situations more effectively.

Happy individuals tend to be more resilient and capable of coping positively with stress. Happiness helps people develop emotional skills that enable them to manage life's challenges more effectively. Additionally, happy people often have a positive perspective on life, allowing them to find creative and constructive solutions to problems.

Happiness also contributes to building and maintaining healthy social relationships, providing a strong support system during stressful times. Having trusted individuals to rely on can reduce the impact of stress on mental and physical health.

Happiness is not only a promoter of resilience and positive stress coping but also has beneficial effects on physical and mental health. Research has shown that happiness directly impacts quality of life, longevity, and disease prevention.

For instance, studies have found that happy individuals are at lower risk of developing chronic illnesses such as diabetes, cardiovascular disease, or cancer. Happiness is also linked to faster recovery from illnesses. Optimistic and happy individuals typically have stronger immune systems and lower levels of inflammation.

Additionally, happiness positively affects mental health. Happy people experience less anxiety, depression, and stress. Happiness has also been shown to correlate positively with job satisfaction, social relationships, and overall psychological well-being.

How to Foster Happiness in Our Lives

Happiness is not something that can be achieved passively; it requires intentional and ongoing effort. Some activities that have been shown to promote happiness include physical exercise, meditation, gratitude, developing satisfying social relationships, and engaging in activities we are passionate about.

- **Physical exercise** boosts the production of endorphins, hormones responsible for feelings of well-being. Exercise can also enhance self-esteem and self-confidence, fostering a positive outlook on life.
- **Meditation** has proven effective in reducing stress and anxiety. It helps individuals develop greater awareness of their thoughts and emotions, enabling better management of these feelings.
- **Gratitude** focuses on appreciating what we have rather than what we lack. Practicing gratitude helps us value the positive aspects of our lives and focus on what we cherish.
- **Developing satisfying social relationships** provides a sense of belonging and emotional support. Feeling connected and supported by others contributes to

greater happiness and resilience.
- **Engaging in activities we are passionate about** gives us a sense of purpose and fulfillment. These activities help us find meaning in life and foster a sense of achievement and satisfaction.

In summary, happiness is an emotional state that promotes resilience and positive stress coping while also providing numerous physical and mental health benefits. Cultivating happiness requires intentional and ongoing effort through practices such as physical exercise, meditation, gratitude, building strong social connections, and pursuing passions.

Chapter 4: What Prevents Us From Being Happy?

Even though happiness is something we all want in our lives, we often find ourselves trapped in a state of dissatisfaction, stress, and discouragement that prevents us from achieving the happiness we desire so much. This lack of happiness can manifest in many different ways, from the inability to enjoy the present to a constant feeling of emptiness that makes us feel disconnected from the world around us.

It is important to understand that there are many factors that can contribute to the lack of happiness in our lives. In some cases, it may be a matter of external circumstances, such as an unsatisfying job situation or a toxic relationship that makes us feel trapped and hopeless. In other cases, the problem may be an internal one, such as the constant pressure we put on ourselves to be perfect or the lack of sense or purpose in our lives.

One of the main barriers that prevent us from being happy is the chronic stress we often experience in our lives. Constant stress can affect our physical and mental health and make us feel overwhelmed, distressed, and discouraged. In addition, stress can make us focus only on the negative aspects of our lives, preventing us from finding happiness in those moments that should bring us joy.

Another important barrier that prevents us from being happy is emotional trauma, as painful experiences from the past can make it difficult to find happiness in our daily lives.

Trauma can make us feel disconnected from the world around us and struggle to find meaning and purpose in our lives.

The lack of social support is also an important barrier that can hinder our pursuit of happiness. Satisfying social relationships are crucial for our happiness and general well-being, and when we find ourselves disconnected from others, we can feel isolated and lonely, which affects our mental health and makes it harder to find happiness.

Constant comparison with others is another barrier that prevents us from being happy. The world we live in constantly pressures us to be more successful, richer, more attractive, and more accomplished than others. This constant comparison can make us feel like we are in constant competition with others, preventing us from finding happiness in our own lives.

Finally, the lack of purpose or meaning in life is another barrier that prevents us from being happy. When we do not have a clear sense of what we want in life or do not feel that we are making a meaningful contribution to the world around us, we can feel lost and directionless. This can make us feel that our life lacks purpose or meaning, preventing us from finding happiness in our daily lives.

In summary, although happiness is something we all want in our lives, there are many barriers that can make our pursuit of happiness difficult. From chronic stress to emotional trauma, the lack of social support, constant comparison with others, and the lack of purpose or meaning in life, these barriers can make us feel trapped and hopeless. However, by understanding these barriers and working to overcome them, we can find the happiness we desire so much and improve our overall well-being.

Internal Barriers That Prevent Us From Being Happy

In addition to the external barriers mentioned above, there are also internal barriers that prevent us from being happy. These barriers are related to our own minds and thoughts and can include negative thinking, self-criticism, and excessive self-demand.

Negative thoughts are those that make us focus on bad things and see the negative in any situation. These thoughts may be rooted in our own insecurity and fear of failure or criticism. When we focus on the negative, our brain releases certain hormones and neurotransmitters that make us feel stressed, anxious, and unhappy.

Self-criticism is another type of internal barrier that prevents us from being happy. Self-criticism occurs when we are too harsh on ourselves and constantly judge everything we do. This can lead to a lack of self-esteem and confidence, which affects our ability to find happiness. Instead of being compassionate and kind to ourselves, we constantly punish ourselves for our mistakes.

Excessive self-demand is also an internal barrier that prevents us from being happy. Self-demand happens when we set standards that are too high for ourselves and strive to reach unrealistic goals. This can lead to frustration and a constant sense of failure. Instead of celebrating our achievements, we focus on what remains to be done.

It is important to recognize these internal barriers and work to overcome them. This may include practicing self-compassion, accepting our mistakes, and being kinder to ourselves. We can also learn to challenge our negative thoughts and set more realistic and achievable goals. By doing so, we can find the happiness and well-being we so deeply desire.

There are several internal barriers that can prevent us from being happy, including:

1. **Negative thoughts:** Negative thoughts can sabotage our happiness. When we focus on the negative in a situation or in ourselves, they make us feel bad and hinder our ability to enjoy the present.
2. **Self-criticism:** Excessive self-criticism can make us feel insufficient and devalued, which in turn can cause anxiety and depression. It is important to recognize our mistakes and flaws, but it is also essential to be compassionate and kind to ourselves.
3. **Excessive self-demand:** Excessive self-demand leads us to set unrealistic expectations for ourselves and our lives, which can create stress and frustration. It is important to be ambitious and have goals, but it is also crucial to accept our limitations and value what we have.
4. **Fear of change:** Fear of change can prevent us from exploring new opportunities and experiences that could make us happy. It is important to learn to step out of our comfort zone and be open to new possibilities.
5. **Lack of acceptance:** The lack of acceptance of ourselves and others can generate resentment and conflict. It is important to learn to accept ourselves as we are and others in their diversity.

6. **Perfectionism:** Perfectionism can prevent us from enjoying our achievements and make us feel constantly dissatisfied. It is important to learn to value the process and effort, not just the final results.

In summary, identifying and working on our internal barriers can be essential to achieving happiness and emotional well-being.

External Barriers That Prevent Us From Being Happy

Happiness is an emotional state desired by everyone, yet we often face external factors that prevent us from achieving it. Among these external barriers are stress, emotional trauma, lack of social support, constant comparison with others, and lack of purpose or meaning in life.

Stress is an external barrier that prevents us from being happy. Stress leads us to feel overwhelmed, tense, and out of control. Stress is a natural response of the body to situations perceived as threatening or challenging. However, chronic stress is harmful to our physical and mental health and can be an obstacle to achieving happiness.

Emotional trauma is another external barrier that often prevents us from being happy. Emotional trauma can result from traumatic situations such as violence, war, bullying, or abuse. Emotional trauma can have long-lasting effects that prevent us from feeling happy and secure in our lives and relationships.

A lack of social support is also an external barrier that prevents us from being happy. Quality interpersonal relationships are essential for our emotional health and well-being. Without a strong social network, we may feel lonely, isolated, and disconnected, which hinders our ability to achieve happiness.

Constant comparison with others is another external barrier that prevents us from being happy. When we constantly compare ourselves to others, we focus on our limitations and feel inadequate. Constant comparison can lead to anxiety, depression, and low self-esteem.

Finally, a lack of purpose or meaning in life is another external barrier that prevents us from being happy. When we lack a clear vision of our life's purpose, we may feel lost and directionless. A lack of purpose or meaning in life can lead to apathy, lack of motivation, and unhappiness.

It is important to recognize these external barriers and work to overcome them. We can learn to manage stress, seek professional help to address emotional trauma, nurture our social relationships, stop comparing ourselves to others, and find purpose and meaning in life. By doing so, we can free ourselves from the external barriers that prevent us from being happy and achieve a fulfilling and satisfying life.

Some of These External Barriers Include:

1. **Stressful and Anxiety-Inducing Situations:** Stress and anxiety can affect our ability to be happy and enjoy life. Situations such as financial problems, work or family conflicts, or risky circumstances can

generate high levels of stress and anxiety that impact our emotional health.
2. **Negative Social Environment:** A negative social environment can be an external barrier to our happiness. Being surrounded by toxic, critical, or unsupportive people can make us feel bad and hinder our ability to achieve happiness.
3. **Precarious Living Conditions:** Precarious living conditions, such as homelessness, limited access to healthcare or education, or insecurity, can make it difficult for us to be happy and reach our potential.
4. **Discrimination and Prejudice:** Discrimination and prejudice can negatively affect our self-esteem and our ability to feel valued and accepted. Discrimination can take various forms, such as racism, homophobia, sexism, or religious intolerance.
5. **Lack of Opportunities:** Lack of opportunities, such as unemployment, limited access to education, or scarce resources, can hinder our ability to achieve our goals and feel fulfilled.

In conclusion, there are many external barriers that can impede our happiness and emotional well-being. Identifying these barriers and working to overcome them can be essential to achieving the happiness we deserve.

Strategies to Overcome Barriers and Foster Happiness

Happiness is an emotional state that can be affected by various barriers, such as stress, anxiety, lack of motivation, among others. To foster happiness, it is essential to identify these barriers and apply strategies to overcome them. Below are some strategies to overcome barriers and foster happiness:

Life can present various barriers that, in many cases, prevent us from achieving the happiness we desire. However, there are strategies we can apply to overcome these barriers and live a happier and more fulfilling life. Here are some of these strategies:

1. **Practice Gratitude:** Often, we focus so much on what we don't have or don't like that we forget to value and appreciate what we do have. Practicing gratitude means focusing on the positive, recognizing the good things in our lives, and being thankful for them. This helps us gain a more positive perspective on life and feel happier.
2. **Learn to Manage Stress:** Stress can be a significant barrier to happiness, as it can drain us and make us feel overwhelmed. To overcome this barrier, it is important to learn how to manage stress and find ways to relax and reduce anxiety. This may include practicing calming activities such as meditation, yoga, or simply taking a walk outdoors.
3. **Cultivate Positive Relationships:** Social relationships are fundamental in our lives and can be

HAPPINESS: AN ANALYSIS OF A DESIRE

a great source of happiness. Therefore, it is important to cultivate positive and healthy relationships, surround ourselves with people who support us and make us feel good. This may include making new friends, joining groups with shared interests, or simply spending quality time with family and friends.
4. **Learn to Accept and Love Ourselves:** Often, our own attitude toward ourselves can be a major barrier to happiness. If we constantly criticize ourselves and are overly harsh, it's difficult to feel happy and satisfied. That's why it's important to learn to accept and love ourselves, recognize our strengths and weaknesses, and be kinder and more compassionate with ourselves.
5. **Set Goals and Work Toward Them:** Having a purpose in life is essential for feeling happy and fulfilled. Therefore, it's important to set goals that motivate us and work toward achieving them. Whether it's learning a new language, traveling to a place we've always wanted to visit, or getting a new job, having a clear objective helps us feel more focused and happy.
6. **Maintain Regular Physical Activity:** Physical exercise not only helps us stay healthy but is also an excellent way to reduce stress and improve our mood. Exercise releases endorphins that make us feel happier and more energized. Additionally, having a healthy and fit body boosts our self-confidence and makes us feel more secure.
7. **Develop Resilience:** Resilience is the ability to face

and overcome the challenges and obstacles that life presents us. By developing this skill, we can overcome adversity more easily and maintain a positive attitude in the face of difficulties. To develop resilience, it's important to see problems as opportunities, seek creative solutions, and rely on the support of loved ones.

8. **Practice Empathy and Compassion:** Often, the biggest barrier to our happiness is the lack of connection with others. To overcome this barrier, it's important to learn to put ourselves in others' shoes, understand their problems and needs, and treat them with compassion and respect. Practicing empathy and compassion enhances our ability to love and be loved.

9. **Enjoy the Present Moment:** Many times, we worry so much about the future or cling so tightly to the past that we miss out on the present moment. However, the present moment is all we truly have. To enjoy it, it's important to learn to be present in the here and now, cultivate mindfulness, and appreciate life's simple pleasures.

10. **Find Meaning and Purpose in Life:** Finally, to foster happiness in our lives, it's important to find meaning and purpose in our existence. This means identifying activities that ignite our passions and make us feel alive and fulfilled, and dedicating ourselves to them with commitment and enthusiasm. By finding a purpose in life, we can derive meaning and satisfaction from our actions and live a happier and more fulfilling life.

Chapter 5: Strategies to Cultivate Happiness

Happiness is an emotional state desired by everyone, but it is often difficult to achieve and maintain consistently. Therefore, this chapter focuses on providing practical and effective tools to help people enhance their emotional well-being and improve their quality of life. Through these strategies, individuals can learn to develop healthy and positive habits that promote long-term happiness, even during times of adversity or stress.

There are various techniques and practices we can apply to work on emotional well-being and foster happiness. Some of them include:

1. **Meditation:** Meditation is a practice that helps us cultivate mindfulness and reduce stress and anxiety. By practicing meditation regularly, we can calm our minds and connect with our inner selves, helping us find the peace and serenity necessary to be happy.
2. **Visualization:** Visualization is a technique that involves imagining positive and pleasant situations, such as a place of rest or a scenario where we feel happy and fulfilled. By visualizing these situations, we can create positive emotions and generate a sense of emotional well-being.
3. **Physical Exercise:** Physical exercise not only helps us stay in shape but is also an excellent way to reduce stress and improve our mood. When we exercise, we

release endorphins, which are hormones that make us feel happier and more energized.
4. **Humor:** Having a good sense of humor and learning to find the humorous side of situations, as well as being able to laugh at ourselves, can be an effective practice. This helps us reduce stress and anxiety while cultivating positive emotions such as joy and optimism.
5. **Therapy:** Therapy is an excellent way to work on emotional well-being, as it allows us to explore our emotions and thoughts and learn tools to manage difficult situations and improve our relationships with ourselves and others.
6. **Conscious Breathing:** Conscious breathing involves paying attention to our breath and maintaining a calm, deep rhythm. This technique can help us reduce stress and anxiety and improve both emotional and physical well-being.
7. **Gratitude:** Gratitude is a practice that involves focusing on the positive aspects of our lives and feeling thankful for them. By practicing gratitude, we can cultivate positive emotions such as joy, satisfaction, and optimism.
8. **Creativity:** Creativity is an excellent way to work on emotional well-being, as it allows us to express ourselves authentically and release our emotions healthily. This can include activities such as painting, writing, music, dancing, and more.
9. **Contact with Nature:** Connecting with nature can have a positive impact on our emotional and physical

well-being, as it allows us to disconnect from daily routines and connect with something greater than ourselves.

10. **Socialization:** Socialization is important for emotional well-being, as it allows us to connect with others and feel part of a community. This can include activities like meeting friends, joining interest groups, or taking classes.

Promoting Positive Interpersonal Relationships

In today's society, interpersonal relationships are one of the fundamental pillars of well-being, growth, and personal fulfillment. Humans are inherently social beings who establish bonds with others to share, support, and develop themselves. In this sense, fostering positive interpersonal relationships is a key factor in achieving happiness and success in life.

To build positive interpersonal relationships, it is important to have a deep understanding of ourselves to grasp how our actions and behaviors affect others. It is also necessary to recognize and accept differences and diversity in others and learn to respect and appreciate the unique perspectives that each individual brings.

Here are strategies to foster positive interpersonal relationships:

1. **Practice Empathy and Compassion:** Empathy is the ability to put yourself in someone else's shoes and understand their situation and perspective.

Compassion is the capacity to understand someone else's suffering and strive to help them. By practicing empathy and compassion, we create a supportive and respectful environment that allows for the development of positive and meaningful relationships.
2. **Learn Effective Communication:** Communication is fundamental to establishing positive interpersonal relationships. Learning to listen actively, express our ideas clearly, and use non-violent language is key to avoiding misunderstandings and conflicts.
3. **Create Spaces for Inclusion:** A sense of belonging is essential for creating positive interpersonal relationships. By creating spaces that promote inclusion, collaboration, and respect for diversity, we build an environment conducive to the creation of positive interpersonal relationships.
4. **Develop Social Skills:** Social skills enable us to interact effectively with others. Learning to manage our emotions, work as part of a team, make decisions, and solve problems are skills that contribute to building healthy and positive interpersonal relationships.
5. **Engage in Acts of Kindness:** Acts of kindness are those that aim to benefit others and contribute to building a better society. By engaging in acts of kindness, we create bonds of trust and respect that nurture positive interpersonal relationships.
6. **Accept and Respect Differences:** Diversity is a reality in our society, and it is important to learn to

accept and respect it. Recognizing cultural, gender, religious, and other differences and appreciating the richness they bring is key to building positive interpersonal relationships and avoiding conflict.

7. **Practice Gratitude:** Recognizing and appreciating what others do for us, whether big or small, helps create an atmosphere of appreciation and respect. Additionally, practicing gratitude makes us aware of the importance of interpersonal relationships in our lives and motivates us to care for and nurture them.

8. **Maintain an Open and Flexible Attitude:** Interpersonal relationships are constantly evolving, and it is important to be willing to adapt and modify how we relate to improve them. Maintaining an open and flexible attitude toward situations and changes allows us to learn and grow together.

9. **Foster Collaboration and Teamwork:** Collaboration and teamwork allow us to share efforts, ideas, and resources to achieve common goals. Working together strengthens and builds positive interpersonal relationships based on trust, cooperation, and respect.

10. **Value and Care for Interpersonal Relationships:** Interpersonal relationships are important and require attention and care to remain healthy. It is essential to dedicate time and effort to maintain, nurture, and strengthen them, whether through meetings, conversations, acts of kindness, or other means.

11. **Practice Active Listening:** Effective communication is essential for establishing positive interpersonal

relationships. Ensure you actively listen to the other person, paying attention to what they are saying without judging or interrupting. Ask questions to show interest and understanding.
12. **Be Honest and Authentic:** Honesty and authenticity are essential for establishing lasting and meaningful interpersonal relationships.

Promoting Activities and Hobbies That Make Us Happy

Modern life can be stressful and hectic, and we often find ourselves consumed by responsibilities and tasks that leave little time for the things we truly enjoy. However, it's important to remember that dedicating time to activities and hobbies that make us happy can have a positive impact on our health and well-being.

When we engage in activities we enjoy and that make us feel good, our bodies release endorphins and other chemicals that improve our mood and reduce stress levels. Additionally, when we take pleasure in what we do, our minds relax, and we feel more connected to ourselves and to others.

Promoting activities and hobbies that bring us happiness is essential for maintaining balance in our lives and preventing depression and other emotional disorders. Moreover, when we devote time to what we love, we become more creative and productive in other areas of our lives.

In summary, dedicating time to activities and hobbies that make us happy is a valuable investment in our health and

HAPPINESS: AN ANALYSIS OF A DESIRE

well-being, and we should make every effort to find time for these activities in our daily lives.

Below are a series of recommendations for activities and hobbies:

1. **Playing Sports:** Physical exercise releases endorphins, which can make us feel happier and reduce stress. Additionally, it helps us stay fit and healthy. You can look for a sport you enjoy or simply go for a walk or a run.
2. **Listening to Music:** Music has a very positive impact on our mood. Listening to your favorite songs or discovering new artists can be an excellent way to relax and brighten your day.
3. **Cooking:** For many people, cooking is a therapeutic and rewarding activity. You can search for new recipes and experiment with different ingredients to create delicious dishes.
4. **Painting or Drawing:** Art can be a creative and relaxing way to express yourself. You can explore different techniques and styles to discover which ones you like the most.
5. **Meditating:** Meditation can help reduce stress and anxiety and improve our concentration and focus. You can find online meditation guides or simply sit in a quiet place and breathe deeply.
6. **Playing Sports Again:** Physical activity is emphasized because of its multiple benefits. Find a sport you enjoy, or take a walk or jog for both physical and emotional benefits.

7. **Reading:** Reading can be a relaxing and entertaining activity. Choosing a good book can transport us to imaginary places and help us disconnect from daily worries.
8. **Learning a New Language:** Speaking a new language opens many doors, new experiences, and allows us to understand and interact with people from other countries and cultures.
9. **Traveling:** Discovering new destinations, learning more about the history and culture of the world enriches our lives and allows us to enjoy each day more.

By incorporating these activities into our lives, we can enhance our well-being, maintain emotional balance, and cultivate happiness.

Fostering Resilience and Positive Adaptation to Change

Resilience and positive adaptation to change are important skills for tackling life's challenges. Resilience refers to a person's ability to face and overcome adverse situations, while positive adaptation to change involves the capacity to adjust to changes in life constructively and without losing optimism.

Fostering resilience and positive adaptation to change is fundamental for our mental and emotional health, as it enables us to successfully navigate difficult situations and adapt to new circumstances. In an ever-changing world, these skills are increasingly important for our ability to thrive and grow.

HAPPINESS: AN ANALYSIS OF A DESIRE

To foster resilience and positive adaptation to change, it is essential to develop flexible thinking, an open attitude towards new ideas and changes in your environment, and to seek support from close social relationships. These factors can help address stressful situations more effectively.

To cultivate resilience and positive adaptation to change, it is important to develop flexible thinking, an open attitude towards new ideas and changes in our environment, and to seek support from close social relationships. These factors can help address stressful situations more effectively.

An example of fostering resilience could be someone who, after losing their job, chooses to update their skills and knowledge to be better prepared for future job opportunities. Another example might be someone who, after a divorce, focuses on the future and works on establishing effective communication with their ex-partner to ensure a better quality of life for both parties.

In this context, it is crucial to identify strategies and tools that allow us to develop these abilities and to practice them regularly to strengthen them. Education, social support, and self-reflection are valuable tools that can help us build resilience and enhance our ability to adapt positively to change.

Fostering resilience and positive adaptation to change involves developing a series of skills that enable us to effectively face life's difficulties with an optimistic attitude. Below are some strategies to promote these abilities:

1. **Develop Self-Awareness:** Self-awareness is crucial for identifying our strengths and weaknesses and for recognizing our thought and behavior patterns.

When we are aware of our thoughts and emotions, we can develop effective strategies to handle difficult situations and adapt to changes. A tool to enhance self-awareness is meditation, which allows us to connect more deeply with our thoughts and emotions.

2. **Cultivate Supportive Relationships:** Social relationships can be a vital source of emotional support and practical help during crises. Maintaining a strong and meaningful support network can help us face challenges more effectively and adapt to changes more positively. An example of fostering supportive relationships could be participating in community groups or activities that share our interests and values.
3. **Practice Problem-Solving:** Problem-solving is an essential skill for addressing difficult situations and finding effective solutions. Practicing this skill can enhance our ability to tackle challenges more effectively and positively. An example of a problem-solving tool is situation analysis, which breaks down a problem into smaller parts to address it more effectively.
4. **Learn New Skills:** Acquiring new skills can be an effective way to develop resilience and the ability to adapt positively to change. By learning new skills, we expand our knowledge and capabilities, enabling us to face new challenges with greater confidence and ability.
5. **Practice Self-Reflection:** Self-reflection helps us identify our strengths and weaknesses and become

more aware of our thoughts and emotions. This awareness allows us to develop a more positive attitude towards challenges.
6. **Build a Social Support Network:** Having friends and family we can rely on in difficult times helps us face life's challenges more effectively. Support groups or therapy can also be valuable resources.
7. **Learn to Embrace Change:** Instead of resisting change, it is important to learn to adapt positively. This means accepting that change is inevitable and focusing on finding solutions rather than lamenting what has changed.
8. **Cultivate Emotional Resilience:** Emotional resilience involves learning to manage stress and negative emotions effectively. This can be achieved through meditation, relaxation techniques, physical exercise, and other stress-reducing practices.
9. **Practice Daily Gratitude:** Taking a few minutes each day to think about what we are grateful for helps maintain a positive attitude towards life.
10. **Seek New Opportunities:** Instead of clinging to what we already know, it is important to remain open to new experiences and opportunities.
11. **Learn from Negative Experiences:** Rather than viewing negative experiences as failures, we can seek lessons in them and view them as opportunities for growth.

By implementing these strategies, we can build the resilience and adaptability needed to navigate life's challenges and maintain a positive and constructive outlook.

Chapter 6: Relationships and Happiness

Interpersonal relationships are a fundamental part of our lives and can significantly impact our emotional well-being. From family and friends to romantic partners and colleagues, our relationships play a vital role in how we feel about ourselves and life in general. In this chapter, we will examine the benefits of having healthy and positive relationships, explore ways to improve our communication skills, and strengthen our interpersonal connections. We will also address some common challenges in relationships, such as conflicts and lack of communication, and offer strategies to overcome them.

The Importance of Human Connection for Happiness

Human connection is essential for our happiness and emotional well-being. As social beings, we are wired to connect with others and establish meaningful, healthy relationships in our lives. However, in today's digital age, many people feel increasingly isolated and disconnected, which can have serious consequences for our mental and emotional health.

Meaningful and healthy relationships provide us with a sense of belonging, emotional support, security, and emotional stability. These relationships offer opportunities to share emotional experiences—such as joy, love, pain, and uncertainty—while also allowing us to grow and mature as human beings. Human connection unites us as a species and brings significant physical, mental, and emotional benefits.

When we connect with others, a series of hormones are released in our brains that make us feel good. Oxytocin, often referred to as the "love hormone," is released when we establish meaningful and satisfying relationships. Additionally, other important neurotransmitters, such as dopamine and serotonin, are linked to feelings of happiness and satisfaction, and they are released when we interact with people who matter to us.

Research has shown that people with healthy and meaningful interpersonal relationships experience greater well-being and happiness compared to those who feel isolated or lonely. Human connections provide us with a sense of belonging, purpose, and emotional support, which help us better manage stress and life's challenges.

Having healthy relationships can also improve our physical and mental health. People with positive and meaningful relationships tend to have stronger immune systems and a lower risk of cardiovascular diseases and depression. Furthermore, relationships can boost our self-esteem and confidence, enabling us to make better decisions and maintain a more positive outlook on life.

As we progress through life, our relationships evolve and change, but it is always important to prioritize human connection. This includes strengthening existing relationships, building new connections, and seeking emotional support when needed.

The need for human connection is not a new concept. Since ancient times, humans have had a fundamental need to feel part of something and interact with others. However, today, the quality of our relationships and our ability to connect with others have been significantly impacted by technology and social media.

It's important to note that human connection not only positively influences our happiness but also helps us cope with life's emotional challenges. Meaningful relationships provide emotional support during times of stress and difficulty, making them easier to navigate. Additionally, connecting with others allows us to find comfort and understanding during moments of sadness or grief.

In summary, there is no doubt that human connection is vital for our happiness and emotional well-being. Meaningful and healthy relationships are an endless source of support, security, and love in our lives. In today's digital era, it is crucial to remember the importance of connecting with others and working together to maintain meaningful relationships. By focusing on building and sustaining healthy and satisfying relationships, we can experience a profound sense of happiness and fulfillment in our lives.

Why Human Connection Is Crucial for Our Happiness

Here are some reasons why human connection is so essential to our happiness:

1. **Improves Mental Health**: People with positive and meaningful social relationships tend to have better mental and emotional health. Human connection gives us a sense of purpose and meaning in life,

which, in turn, can enhance our self-esteem and confidence.
2. **Increases Resilience**: Having people who support us during tough times can help us overcome adversities more easily. Human connection provides opportunities to share our experiences and emotions with others, which can strengthen our emotional resilience and coping abilities.
3. **Reduces Stress**: Human connection can help reduce stress and anxiety. Simply being in the presence of another person can be comforting, and having someone to talk to about our problems and concerns can help us find solutions and feel more secure.
4. **Promotes a Sense of Community**: Human connection ties us to others and makes us feel part of something greater than ourselves. This can enhance our sense of belonging and purpose in life.

It's important to remember that human connection isn't just about having numerous relationships; it's about having healthy and meaningful ones. We may not have a large number of friends, but if we cultivate a few close and authentic relationships, we can experience many of the benefits that human connection brings.

Strategies for Improving Interpersonal Relationships

Interpersonal relationships are fundamental to our emotional and physical well-being and can significantly influence our

HAPPINESS: AN ANALYSIS OF A DESIRE

happiness. Having healthy and fulfilling relationships with friends, family, and coworkers can enhance our quality of life, reduce stress, and increase our sense of belonging and connection with others. However, maintaining positive interpersonal relationships can sometimes be challenging, especially when we face conflicts or life difficulties. For this reason, it is essential to develop skills and strategies to improve our interpersonal relationships and, in turn, promote happiness in our lives. Below are several strategies that can be implemented to enhance interpersonal relationships and foster happiness:

1. **Practice Empathy**: Putting yourself in someone else's shoes can help you understand their feelings and perspectives. Actively listen and show genuine interest in their concerns and opinions.
2. **Communicate Clearly**: Effective communication is key to building healthy relationships. Ensure that you express your thoughts and feelings clearly and respectfully, avoiding confrontation and aggression.
3. **Practice Gratitude**: Show appreciation for what others do for you, and acknowledge their efforts and achievements. Gratitude is an essential component of happiness and can foster positivity in interpersonal relationships.
4. **Cultivate Trust**: Be honest and transparent in your relationships. Trust is fundamental to building lasting and satisfying connections.
5. **Resolve Conflicts Constructively**: Conflicts are inevitable in any relationship, but how you handle

them matters. Strive to resolve conflicts constructively by listening to the other person and working together to find solutions that satisfy both parties.
6. **Practice Patience**: Relationships require time and effort to grow. Be patient and tolerant with others, especially when they are facing difficulties or personal problems.
7. **Find Shared Activities**: Discover activities you can enjoy together, whether it's a sport, hobby, or project. This can help strengthen bonds and improve communication.
8. **Embrace Diversity**: Recognize and value cultural and personal differences. Foster diversity and strive to learn from others, opening your mind to new perspectives and ways of seeing the world.

How to Avoid Social Isolation and Loneliness

Loneliness and social isolation are problems that can affect people of all ages and have serious consequences for mental and physical health. Social isolation refers to the lack of social interaction with others, while loneliness refers to a sense of emotional isolation, even when surrounded by people. Both issues can significantly impact a person's quality of life and are especially common among older adults, though they can also affect young people and adults at different points in life.

Loneliness and social isolation can be linked to various factors, such as a lack of social skills, the loss of loved ones,

HAPPINESS: AN ANALYSIS OF A DESIRE

changes in work life or retirement, chronic illnesses or disabilities, and lack of access to transportation or community services. The effects of loneliness and social isolation can be severe, including mental health issues like depression, anxiety, stress, and sleep disorders. Loneliness and social isolation have also been shown to impact physical health, increasing the risk of cardiovascular diseases, obesity, diabetes, and other chronic health problems.

It is essential to note that loneliness and social isolation are not the same. Social isolation refers to the lack of social contact, while loneliness refers to a subjective feeling of emotional isolation. Therefore, it is possible to feel lonely even when surrounded by people, and conversely, to lack social contact but not feel lonely. Moreover, loneliness is not inherently negative, as it can signal a need for more social interaction in a person's life.

Fortunately, many strategies can be used to avoid social isolation and loneliness. One of the main strategies is participating in social activities. This can include joining interest groups, clubs, or community activities that allow people to meet new individuals and build meaningful social relationships. Maintaining contact with friends and family is also crucial, as it can provide an emotional support network and a sense of connection.

Volunteering is another effective way to combat loneliness and social isolation. Volunteering can provide a sense of purpose and meaning and is an excellent way to connect with the community and meet new people. Recreational activities can also help avoid social isolation and loneliness. Participating in sports, yoga, dance, or other recreational activities can provide a sense of accomplishment and improve physical and emotional health.

In addition to these strategies, it is essential to seek professional help if you are dealing with feelings of loneliness and social isolation. A counselor or therapist can provide tools to improve social skills and help you connect with your community. Practicing self-compassion can also be an effective tool to reduce feelings of loneliness and social isolation.

Strategies to Combat Social Isolation and Loneliness

1. **Participate in Social Activities**: Joining social activities is an excellent way to avoid social isolation and loneliness. Consider joining an interest group, club, or community organization. These opportunities allow you to meet new people and build meaningful relationships.
2. **Maintain Contact with Friends and Family**: Keeping in touch with friends and family is crucial to avoid social isolation and loneliness. Stay connected regularly through phone calls, emails, or video chats, especially if you live far away from them.
3. **Volunteer**: Volunteering is a great way to connect with the community and meet new people. Look for volunteer opportunities in your area and join a group that aligns with your interests.
4. **Engage in Recreational Activities**: Participating in recreational activities such as sports, yoga, or dance is an excellent way to meet new people and build

meaningful social relationships. Recreational activities can also improve physical and emotional health.

5. **Adopt a Pet**: Having a pet can be an effective way to combat loneliness and social isolation. Pets provide companionship and emotional support and can also motivate you to leave the house and exercise.
6. **Learn Something New**: Learning something new can be an excellent way to meet people and build meaningful relationships. Consider taking online or in-person classes in areas of interest that offer opportunities to connect with others.
7. **Seek Professional Help**: If you are struggling with feelings of loneliness and social isolation, it is essential to seek professional help. A counselor or therapist can provide tools to improve your social skills and help you connect with your community.
8. **Practice Self-Compassion**: Practicing self-compassion can help reduce feelings of loneliness and social isolation. Self-compassion involves being kind and understanding toward yourself and accepting yourself as you are.
9. **Take Care of Physical Health**: Taking care of your physical health is essential to avoid social isolation and loneliness. Try to exercise regularly, get enough sleep, eat a healthy diet, and avoid substance abuse.
10. **Participate in Online Activities**: Social media and other online platforms can be great ways to connect with like-minded people and build meaningful social relationships. Join online groups, participate in

discussion forums, and share your interests with others online.

Chapter 7: Happiness at Work

Happiness at work is an increasingly important topic in the corporate and professional world. Happiness at work refers to a person's ability to experience positive emotions in relation to their job and work environment. People who experience happiness at work tend to be more productive, creative, and engaged in their work, which can lead to better performance and greater job satisfaction. On the other hand, a lack of happiness at work can lead to problems such as stress, demotivation, lack of commitment, and job dissatisfaction.

Happiness at work has become a topic of interest in the corporate and professional world due to the benefits it can offer both employees and companies. Businesses are beginning to recognize that happiness at work is important not only for employee well-being but also for long-term productivity and profitability.

Additionally, employees are paying more attention to happiness at work. With the growing concern for work-life balance, employees are looking for jobs that provide them with a sense of purpose, a positive work environment, and the opportunity to develop their skills and talents. Happiness at work is a key factor for employees when considering a job and can influence their commitment to the company and their long-term retention.

There are various strategies to promote happiness at work. First, it is important for company leaders and managers to commit to creating a positive work environment and a culture that fosters happiness at work. This can include recognizing employees' achievements and efforts, encouraging collaboration, and ensuring open and transparent communication.

It is also important to provide employees with opportunities to develop their skills and talents. Employees who have the chance to learn and grow in their roles tend to feel more engaged and satisfied with their work. Moreover, the possibility of receiving constructive feedback and regular performance reviews can also help employees feel more valued and connected to their work.

Another strategy to foster happiness at work is to promote a healthy work-life balance. Employees who feel they have time for their interests and activities outside of work tend to be happier and more productive at work. This can include flexible scheduling options, paid vacations, and allowing remote work.

Additionally, promoting a culture of well-being and self-care can have a significant impact on happiness at work. Companies can offer wellness programs that encourage physical activity, healthy eating, and stress management. They can also provide access to counseling programs and mental health resources.

Social connection and relationships with coworkers are important factors in workplace happiness. Companies can foster camaraderie and social connections by organizing team events, extracurricular activities, and promoting social interaction among employees. This can improve collaboration, communication, and the sense of community in the workplace.

Finally, it is important to remember that happiness at work is a continuous and dynamic process. Companies and employees must be willing to adapt and evolve to maintain a positive and satisfying work environment. This can include regularly reviewing company policies and practices, gathering employee feedback, and implementing changes as necessary.

How Workplace Happiness Relates to Performance and Satisfaction

Happiness at work is a crucial factor that influences employee performance and satisfaction. Employees who are happy in their jobs are more likely to be productive, maintain a positive attitude, and stay in their roles longer. In this regard, workplace happiness has become a priority for companies seeking to enhance productivity and retain top talent.

Firstly, happiness at work is closely linked to employee performance. Employees who are happy in their jobs tend to be more motivated and committed to their tasks. Studies have shown that happy employees are 12% more productive than unhappy ones, highlighting that workplace happiness can significantly impact a company's performance.

Moreover, happy employees are more likely to be creative and innovative. Creativity is a vital factor in the success of many companies and organizations, and happiness at work can be a key driver of creativity and innovation. Happy employees are more confident in their work and their ability to generate new and innovative ideas.

Workplace happiness is also associated with employee satisfaction. Happy employees are more likely to be satisfied with their jobs and their overall lives. Job satisfaction has been linked to employee retention, meaning that happy employees are more inclined to stay in their roles for extended periods.

This can be advantageous for companies, as employee turnover can be costly in terms of both time and resources.

Additionally, workplace happiness is tied to the mental health and well-being of employees. Happy employees are less likely to experience stress and work-related illnesses. This can lead to a more positive and healthy work environment, which in turn fosters higher performance and greater employee satisfaction.

On the other hand, unhappy employees are more likely to be absent or demonstrate low productivity. Unhappiness at work can stem from various factors, including a negative work environment, lack of recognition and rewards, limited professional development opportunities, and long working hours. Workplace unhappiness can create a toxic and unhealthy environment, which can lead to high employee turnover and diminished productivity.

Strategies to Foster Workplace Happiness

Below are some of the most effective strategies:

1. **Promote a Positive Work Environment**:
   It is essential to create a positive work environment where employees feel valued and appreciated. This can include encouraging collaboration, effective communication, transparency, and honesty, as well as recognizing and rewarding employees' achievements and efforts.
2. **Offer Professional Development Opportunities**:
   Employees who have access to professional

development and growth opportunities are more likely to be satisfied with their jobs. Companies can provide training programs, mentoring, and advancement opportunities to help employees grow in their careers.

3. **Encourage Work-Life Balance**: Work-life balance is vital for employee happiness. Companies can offer flexible working hours, time off, remote work options, and other benefits to help employees balance their professional and personal lives.

4. **Provide a Healthy Work Environment**: Ensuring a healthy and safe work environment for employees is crucial. This may include providing secure and ergonomic facilities, as well as promoting healthy lifestyle habits such as regular physical activity and proper nutrition.

5. **Encourage Collaboration and Teamwork**: Teamwork and collaboration are important for employee well-being and happiness. Companies can encourage collaboration and teamwork through group projects, the creation of task forces, and the organization of social and team-building events.

6. **Provide Benefits and Rewards**: Companies can offer benefits and rewards to motivate employees and improve their workplace happiness. These benefits might include bonuses, incentives, paid vacations, health insurance, and other workplace perks.

7. **Foster Effective Communication**:

IRAYA AHEMÓN GARCÍA

Effective communication is key to employee happiness and well-being. Companies can promote effective communication by organizing regular meetings, providing feedback channels, and fostering a culture of openness and honesty.

Chapter 8: Happiness in the Digital Age

In the digital age we live in, the concept of happiness has evolved and transformed in ways never seen before. The use of technology and access to global information have changed how we interact with the world and with ourselves, impacting how we seek and find happiness.

Technology has made greater connection and communication possible, which can enhance happiness by allowing us to maintain deeper and more meaningful relationships with people around the world. Social media and instant messaging apps have made it easier to stay in touch with friends and family, and technology has enabled people to work from anywhere at any time, leading to greater flexibility and autonomy in the workplace.

On the other hand, the digital age has also resulted in a greater dependence on technology, which can negatively impact happiness. Social media and digital media can create feelings of isolation and loneliness, and excessive time spent online can negatively affect people's mental and emotional health. Additionally, technology has fostered a "always connected" culture, where individuals feel obligated to be constantly available and responsive to messages and emails, disrupting the balance between work and personal life.

Below are some strategies that can help achieve this balance:

1. **Set boundaries:** It's important to establish limits on

technology use to avoid information overload and reduce the feeling of being "always connected." Setting schedules for technology use, turning off notifications, and taking regular screen breaks can help improve work-life balance.
2. **Cultivate meaningful relationships:** Despite the global connectivity that technology provides, it's essential to foster meaningful and close real-life relationships. Taking time to meet in person and connect with friends and family can enhance feelings of connection and reduce isolation.
3. **Practice gratitude:** Gratitude is a powerful strategy for enhancing happiness in any era but is especially important in the digital age. Taking time to appreciate the good things in life and expressing gratitude for relationships and experiences can help maintain a positive and balanced perspective.
4. **Develop digital wellness skills:** It's important to develop skills for digital well-being, including information management, critical evaluation of online information, and online safety. Education on digital wellness skills can help reduce the negative effects of technology on mental and emotional health.
5. **Practice mindfulness:** Practicing mindfulness means being aware and paying attention to what is happening in the present moment without judging or evaluating the experience. In the context of the digital age, this means being mindful of how we use technology and how it affects us emotionally,

cognitively, and physically.

6. **Encourage collaboration and teamwork:** Technology can also be a powerful tool for fostering collaboration and teamwork. Online collaboration tools can help individuals work together more effectively and build stronger team relationships.
7. **Encourage learning and growth:** The digital age has made learning and development more accessible than ever. People can access a variety of online learning resources, from online courses to YouTube tutorials, to improve their skills and knowledge. Encouraging learning and growth in the workplace and personal life can enhance happiness by providing a sense of achievement and purpose.
8. **Practice self-discipline:** In the digital age, self-discipline can be especially important for maintaining happiness and mental health. Practicing self-discipline can help individuals set boundaries on technology use, avoid procrastination, and improve productivity.

How Social Media and Technology Can Affect Our Happiness

Social media and technology can have a significant impact on our happiness. While technology can be a powerful tool for improving communication and connecting with others, it can also negatively impact our mental and emotional health if used excessively or dysfunctionally.

IRAYA AHEMÓN GARCÍA

Social media, in particular, can negatively impact happiness by contributing to social comparison, anxiety, and low self-esteem. Most people present an idealized and edited version of themselves on their social media profiles, which can lead others to compare their lives to an unattainable version of reality. This constant comparison can make individuals feel inadequate or that they are falling short of others' expectations, potentially leading to anxiety and depression.

Furthermore, social media can lead to information overload and a lack of privacy. The amount of information available online can be overwhelming, contributing to increased anxiety and stress. Additionally, social media often requires sharing personal information, increasing vulnerability and reducing privacy.

Another negative effect of technology is constant interruption and distraction. Notifications from our devices can disrupt our work, focus, and ability to be present in the moment. Constant multitasking can also decrease productivity and job satisfaction, ultimately impacting happiness.

However, not everything about technology is negative. Technology can also positively impact happiness by enabling greater connection and communication with others. Social media can be a tool for connecting with friends and family who live far away, and technology can facilitate collaboration and teamwork.

It's important to note that the use of technology itself is neither inherently good nor bad. What matters is how we use it and how it affects our overall life and happiness. Therefore, establishing boundaries and developing digital wellness skills are crucial for fostering a healthy relationship with technology.

Some strategies to foster a healthy relationship with technology include setting limits on usage time, practicing mindfulness and self-regulation, and finding a balance between technology use and offline activities.

Strategies for Using Technology in a Healthy Way to Foster Happiness

The use of technology is an inevitable part of our daily lives in the digital age we live in. Therefore, it is essential to learn how to use technology in a healthy way to promote our happiness and well-being. Below are some strategies that can help achieve this goal:

1. **Set time limits:** One of the best ways to use technology in a healthy way is to set limits on screen time. This means allocating specific time to use technology, such as browsing social media or checking email, and then turning off devices to engage in other offline activities like exercising or socializing in person. Setting time limits can help prevent information overload, fatigue, and technology dependence.
2. **Practice mindfulness:** Mindfulness can help people become more aware of their technology use. Mindfulness involves paying attention to the present moment intentionally and without judgment. By practicing mindfulness, individuals can become more conscious of their technology use and how it affects their well-being. This awareness can help them make

more informed decisions about how to use technology in a healthy way.
3. **Establish boundaries for technology use at work:** It's crucial to set boundaries for technology use in the workplace to avoid constant interruptions and distractions. This may involve turning off notifications or setting specific times to check email or social media. By establishing these boundaries, individuals can improve their productivity and job satisfaction.
4. **Seek a balance between technology use and offline activities:** Finding a balance between technology use and offline activities is essential for fostering happiness. Offline activities, such as exercising, socializing in person, reading books, or engaging in crafts, can help reduce stress and enhance mental and emotional health. Therefore, dedicating time to offline activities is important for maintaining a healthy balance in technology use.
5. **Learn new skills and applications:** Learning new skills and applications can be a fun and enriching way to use technology. This might include learning to code, taking online courses, or downloading meditation or yoga apps. Acquiring new skills and exploring applications can enhance satisfaction and provide a sense of accomplishment, which can contribute to overall happiness.

Chapter 9: Happiness and Health

Happiness and health are intrinsically linked, and it is important to understand how both affect our daily lives. Happiness refers to a general emotional state of well-being, including positive feelings such as joy, gratitude, and life satisfaction. Health, on the other hand, pertains to the overall state of our body and mind, encompassing aspects like physical, mental, and emotional health. Together, happiness and health can significantly enhance our quality of life.

Numerous studies have shown a positive relationship between happiness and health. For instance, research has found that happy people have stronger immune systems and are less likely to develop chronic illnesses such as diabetes, high blood pressure, and heart disease. Additionally, happiness is associated with a lower overall mortality rate. In summary, when we are happy, our body and mind are in better health, and we are more protected against illnesses.

Conversely, health can also influence our happiness. Mental and emotional health, for example, is a vital component of overall health and can significantly impact our emotional well-being. People suffering from anxiety disorders or depression, for instance, may struggle to experience feelings of happiness and joy. Therefore, it is crucial to care for both our physical and mental health to achieve lasting and sustainable happiness.

IRAYA AHEMÓN GARCÍA

How Happiness Relates to Physical and Mental Health

The relationship between happiness and health has been the subject of study in various disciplines for decades. While health is defined as a state of complete physical, mental, and social well-being, happiness refers to a positive emotional state in which individuals experience feelings of joy, satisfaction, and fulfillment in their lives.

Numerous studies have demonstrated a significant relationship between happiness and physical and mental health. In terms of physical health, happiness has been linked to benefits such as reduced risk of cardiovascular diseases, improved immune function, decreased chronic pain, and better sleep quality. Conversely, a lack of happiness has been associated with a higher incidence of chronic illnesses, such as diabetes and hypertension.

Regarding mental health, happiness is linked to overall better mental well-being. Happy people have a lower incidence of mental health disorders, such as depression and anxiety. Happiness is also associated with greater resilience to stress and an enhanced ability to cope with life's stressful situations.

The relationship between happiness and health also works in the opposite direction: good physical and mental health can contribute to happiness. For example, individuals who exercise regularly and follow a healthy diet are at a lower risk of chronic illnesses and have better immune function, which can contribute to greater happiness.

Moreover, mental health plays a crucial role in happiness. People receiving treatment for mental disorders such as depression and anxiety often experience mood improvements and increased overall happiness.

Overall, happiness and health are closely intertwined and influence each other. Thus, it is important for individuals to take steps to improve both their happiness and physical and mental health.

Strategies to Promote Health and Happiness

There are various strategies individuals can implement to foster both health and happiness. Below are some of the most effective strategies:

1. **Engage in regular physical activity:** Regular physical activity is essential for maintaining good physical and mental health. Exercising regularly can help reduce the risk of chronic illnesses, improve sleep, boost energy levels, reduce stress, and enhance mood. It is recommended to engage in at least 150 minutes of moderate physical activity per week, such as walking, running, swimming, or cycling.
2. **Follow a healthy diet:** A healthy diet is critical for maintaining good physical and mental health. It is important to consume a variety of foods, including fruits, vegetables, whole grains, lean proteins, and healthy fats. A nutritious diet can help prevent chronic illnesses, strengthen the immune system, and provide the nutrients needed to maintain good physical and mental health.
3. **Get enough sleep:** Sleep is vital for good physical

and mental health. Lack of sleep can increase the risk of chronic illnesses, decrease concentration and productivity, and negatively affect mood. It is recommended to sleep between 7 and 9 hours each night to maintain good physical and mental health.
4. **Practice mindfulness:** Mindfulness can help individuals become more self-aware, reduce stress, and improve mood. Practicing mindfulness involves paying attention to the present moment without judgment. Mindfulness techniques, such as meditation and mindful breathing, can be highly effective in improving mental and emotional health.
5. **Develop healthy social relationships:** Healthy social relationships are essential for happiness and mental health. Surrounding oneself with positive and supportive people is important. Loneliness can be detrimental to mental and physical health, so it is crucial to seek opportunities to socialize and develop healthy social relationships.
6. **Engage in activities that bring joy:** Activities that bring joy can improve mood and promote happiness. It is important to make time for activities that provide pleasure, such as reading, listening to music, pursuing hobbies, or spending time outdoors.
7. **Seek professional help if needed:** Sometimes, it can be challenging to manage mental and physical health issues on one's own. If an individual is experiencing symptoms of mental or physical disorders, it is important to seek professional help. Health professionals can provide treatment and support to

HAPPINESS: AN ANALYSIS OF A DESIRE

improve mental and physical well-being.

Chapter 10: The Search for Meaning

The search for meaning in life is a crucial aspect of happiness and emotional well-being. People who feel that their lives have purpose and direction tend to be happier and experience less stress and anxiety. Additionally, the pursuit of meaning can help individuals overcome difficult times and find the strength to face challenges and adversity.

The search for meaning involves discovering a purpose in life and a connection to something greater than oneself. It may include engaging in meaningful activities such as working for an important cause, caring for someone in need, or contributing to building a stronger community. It can also involve adopting a philosophy of life that provides guidance and purpose, such as a religious faith or spiritual practice.

The pursuit of meaning is also tied to self-awareness and understanding oneself. Often, people find meaning in life by discovering their strengths and weaknesses, values and beliefs, and goals and aspirations. Reflection and meditation can be valuable tools in exploring these aspects of oneself.

How Finding Purpose and Meaning in Life Can Influence Our Happiness

Finding purpose and meaning in life is a universal human pursuit. It is a personal and subjective process that involves discovering deep and transcendent significance in our experiences, actions, and relationships. Purpose and meaning can vary greatly from person to person, but the sense of finding it can have a profound positive impact on our happiness and well-being.

Research has shown that individuals who have a sense of purpose and meaning in life tend to be happier and healthier both mentally and physically than those who do not. One study found that people who reported having a purpose in life had a significantly lower mortality rate than those who did not. Additionally, individuals with a sense of purpose and meaning are better equipped to handle stress and are more resilient in the face of adversity.

Clearly, having a sense of purpose and meaning in life can influence many aspects of health and well-being. One reason why purpose and meaning can enhance mental health is that they provide direction and motivation. Without understanding why we do what we do, it is easy to feel lost or aimless in life. This can lead to apathy, lack of motivation, and even depression.

On the other hand, when we have a sense of purpose and meaning, we are more likely to have intrinsic motivation to work hard and overcome obstacles. Knowing we are working toward something important gives us a sense of fulfillment and satisfaction. Furthermore, purpose and meaning can help us cope with stress and adversity. When facing difficult situations, we can find comfort in knowing that what we are doing matters and has a purpose, which provides us with strength and resilience.

Finding purpose and meaning in life can also positively impact self-esteem. When we understand what is important to us and work toward those goals, we feel more confident in ourselves and our abilities. Additionally, we may feel more connected to the world around us, which can enhance our happiness and overall well-being.

Physically, studies have found that having a sense of purpose and meaning in life can benefit heart health, the immune system, and sleep quality. When working toward important goals, we are more likely to make healthy choices and take care of ourselves. We are also more inclined to maintain an active lifestyle and avoid harmful behaviors such as smoking or excessive drinking.

Strategies to Find Meaning and Purpose in Life

Finding purpose and meaning in life can be a challenging and deeply personal process, but several strategies can guide individuals on this journey:

1. **Reflect on Values and Passions:** Identifying personal values and activities that bring happiness and fulfillment can be a good starting point for finding purpose and meaning. Making a list of things that are important and meaningful in life and dedicating time to activities that reflect those values can help individuals feel they are living in alignment with their purpose.
2. **Seek New Experiences:** Exploring and discovering new experiences can be an effective way to find purpose and meaning. This might involve traveling, learning something new, engaging in volunteer activities, or even making career changes. These new

experiences can help people uncover new interests and skills, leading to a greater sense of purpose and meaning.
3. **Find Meaning in Suffering:** Suffering is an inevitable part of life, but it can provide opportunities to discover deeper purpose and meaning. Learning to see suffering as an opportunity for growth and development and finding ways to help others facing similar situations can bring new meaning to life.
4. **Connect with Others:** Interpersonal relationships and a sense of community can be sources of purpose and meaning in life. Individuals can seek connections with others through social activities, community groups, or even online forums, allowing them to share experiences and create a sense of belonging and shared purpose.
5. **Pursue Spirituality:** For many people, spiritual exploration is an essential way to find purpose and meaning in life. Meditation, prayer, mindfulness practices, and other spiritual activities can help individuals connect with something greater than themselves and discover a deeper sense of purpose in their lives.

By reflecting on what matters most, exploring new paths, and building meaningful connections, individuals can embark on a fulfilling journey to find purpose and meaning that aligns with their values and enhances their overall well-being.

Chapter 11: Happiness in Different Cultures

Happiness is a universal concept that has been a topic of interest across cultures throughout history. However, the way happiness is defined and pursued varies from one culture to another. Some cultures value individual happiness and the pursuit of personal satisfaction, while others emphasize collective happiness and social harmony.

In many Western cultures, happiness is associated with wealth, success, and the achievement of personal goals. In contrast, in some Eastern cultures, happiness is more related to the acceptance of reality and the pursuit of tranquility and harmony.

Moreover, different religions and philosophies influence how happiness is understood. For instance, Buddhism emphasizes the elimination of suffering through detachment and meditation, while Christianity promotes happiness through connection with God and the practice of charity.

How the Definition and Experience of Happiness Vary Across Cultures

The definition and experience of happiness vary significantly from one culture to another and can be influenced by factors such as religion, tradition, and social beliefs. Below are some examples of how happiness is defined and experienced in different cultures:

1. **Western Culture:** In Western culture, happiness is often associated with success, wealth, and personal fulfillment. Happiness is defined as the ability to achieve personal goals and objectives and feel self-satisfied. In Western culture, happiness is often sought through the consumption of material goods and the pursuit of experiences considered fulfilling, such as travel, leisure activities, and shopping.
2. **Eastern Culture:** In Eastern culture, happiness is often related to tranquility and acceptance of reality. Happiness is defined as the ability to find harmony and inner peace and is sought through meditation and the practice of detachment. In Eastern culture, happiness can also be found through connection with nature and the practice of simple activities, such as gardening.
3. **African Culture:** In African culture, happiness is often associated with connection to the community and family. Happiness is defined as the ability to live in harmony with others and to have purpose and meaning in life. In African culture, happiness can also be found through music, dance, and celebrating life.
4. **Indigenous Culture:** In indigenous cultures, happiness is often connected to nature and the spirits. Happiness is defined as the ability to live in balance with nature and honor ancestors. In indigenous cultures, happiness can also be found through connection with the land, the practice of traditional medicine, and the celebration of sacred rituals.

HAPPINESS: AN ANALYSIS OF A DESIRE

What We Can Learn from Other Cultures About Happiness

Learning from other cultures about happiness can be highly enriching, as it allows us to have a broader and more diverse perspective on this universal concept. Below are some lessons we can learn from other cultures about happiness:

1. **The Importance of Social Relationships:** In many cultures, happiness is tied to connection and harmony with others. We can learn from these cultures the importance of cultivating healthy and meaningful social relationships for our happiness.
2. **The Practice of Gratitude:** In some cultures, happiness lies in the ability to appreciate the simple things in life and be grateful for them. We can learn from these cultures to practice gratitude and value what we have instead of focusing on what we lack.
3. **The Value of Leisure Time:** In some cultures, happiness is associated with the ability to enjoy leisure time and relaxation. We can learn from these cultures to prioritize downtime and rest, finding balance between work and personal life.
4. **Acceptance of Reality:** In some cultures, happiness is linked to the ability to accept reality as it is and find inner peace. We can learn from these cultures to let go of expectations and accept the things we cannot change, focusing instead on what we can control.

IRAYA AHEMÓN GARCÍA

The Importance of a Multidimensional Approach to Happiness

It is important to adopt a multidimensional approach to happiness because the concept of happiness is complex and multifaceted. Happiness is not just about feeling pleasure or satisfaction at a given moment but involves a more comprehensive and profound experience that encompasses the cognitive, emotional, social, and spiritual aspects of life.

For example, a person may feel happy in the moment while eating their favorite dessert, but that does not mean they are happy overall. Long-term happiness also involves having healthy relationships, a meaningful purpose in life, a sense of control and self-determination, and a connection to something greater than oneself.

A multidimensional approach to happiness also recognizes that happiness can vary across different life stages and cultures. What makes one person happy at a given time may not make another person happy at the same time or in a different culture.

Therefore, it is important to be aware of the different dimensions of happiness and consider all of them in our pursuit of happiness and well-being in life. Adopting a multidimensional approach to happiness will enable us to make more informed and strategic decisions about how we can live a happier and more fulfilling life.

Some of the important aspects to consider in a multidimensional approach to happiness include:

1. **Emotional Aspects:** This refers to the subjective experience of happiness, including positive emotions

like joy, gratitude, and love. Emotional happiness also involves the absence of negative emotions such as sadness, anger, and anxiety.
2. **Cognitive Aspects:** This refers to the subjective perception of life in terms of satisfaction and well-being. Cognitive happiness relates to life satisfaction and the perception of personal achievement.
3. **Social Aspects:** This refers to the quality and quantity of social relationships. Social happiness includes having meaningful and fulfilling relationships with friends, family, and the broader community.
4. **Spiritual Aspects:** This refers to connection with something greater than oneself, such as religion, spirituality, or nature. Spiritual happiness involves finding meaning and purpose in life and feeling connected to a greater purpose.

Final Reflections and Recommendations for the Future

The pursuit of happiness is a fundamental part of human life and has been studied across numerous disciplines, including psychology, philosophy, and economics. Throughout this discussion, we have explored how happiness is a subjective and multifaceted concept that varies from person to person and culture to culture.

We have learned that happiness involves emotional, cognitive, social, and spiritual aspects of life and that it is essential to address each of these aspects holistically in our pursuit of happiness and well-being in life.

To achieve greater happiness and well-being, it is important to take time to reflect on our own needs and values and consider how we can integrate them into our daily lives. It is also helpful to adopt a mindful and positive approach, focusing on the present and developing resilience and gratitude.

In terms of recommendations for the future, it is crucial to continue researching and exploring how happiness can be measured and promoted in different cultures and contexts. Additionally, advocating for policies and practices that foster equality, social justice, and collective well-being is fundamental, as these factors are essential for achieving greater happiness and well-being in society as a whole.

Chapter 12: Conclusions

How We Can Apply What We've Learned in Our Daily Lives to Be Happier

Happiness is one of the most studied topics in psychology and philosophy. We all want to be happy, but what is happiness? Is it something that can be measured or objectively defined? Happiness is a subjective concept that varies from person to person and from culture to culture. In the pursuit of happiness, many theories, approaches, and strategies have been developed over time and across different cultures. By understanding how happiness is defined and experienced in various cultural contexts, we can learn valuable lessons about how to live a happier and more fulfilling life.

To apply what we've learned in our daily lives and become happier, we can follow some practical advice:

1. **Cultivate Healthy and Meaningful Social Relationships:** Spend time with friends and family, participate in activities that allow you to meet new people, and make efforts to maintain and improve your existing relationships.
2. **Practice Gratitude:** Every day, take a moment to think about something you are grateful for. It could be something small, like the bright sunshine or a warm cup of coffee, or something bigger, like your job or your home.
3. **Value Leisure Time:** Dedicate time to activities you

enjoy and that help you relax, such as reading, walking outdoors, cooking, or watching a movie. Make sure to balance your leisure time with your daily responsibilities.
4. **Accept Reality:** Learn to let go of things you cannot control and focus on the things you can change. If you are going through a difficult situation, try to shift your perspective and find ways to learn and grow from it.
5. **Practice Meditation or Mindfulness:** Set aside time each day to meditate or practice mindfulness. This will help you focus on the present moment and cultivate a more positive and compassionate attitude toward yourself and others.

Bibliography:

Aristóteles, Ética a Nicómaco.

Brickman, P., Coates, D., & Janoff-Bulman, R. (1978). Lottery winners and accident victims: Is happiness relative? Journal of Personality and Social Psychology, 36(8), 917–927. https://doi.org/10.1037/0022-3514.36.8.917

Cohen, S., Pressman, S. D., & Black, L. L. (2016). Does positive affect influence health?. Psychological Bulletin, 131(6), 925-971.

Chida, Y., & Steptoe, A. (2008). Positive psychological well-being and mortality: A quantitative review of prospective observational studies. Psychosomatic Medicine, 70(7), 741-756.

Davidson, R. J. (2004). Well-being and affective style: neural substrates and biobehavioural correlates. Philosophical Transactions of the Royal Society B: Biological Sciences, 359(1449), 1395-1411.

Diener, E. (2000). Subjective well-being: The science of happiness and a proposal for a national index. American Psychologist, 55(1), 34-43.

Diener, E., Lucas, R. E., & Oishi, S. (2002). Subjective well-being: The science of happiness and life satisfaction. Handbook of Positive Psychology, 63-73.

Diener, E., Lucas, R. E., & Oishi, S. (2018). Advances and open questions in the science of subjective well-being. Collabra: Psychology, 4(1), 15. https://doi.org/10.1525/collabra.115

Epicuro, Carta a Meneceo.

Folkman, S., & Moskowitz, J. T. (2000). Positive affect and the other side of coping. American Psychologist, 55(6), 647-654.

Fredrickson, B. L. (2004). The broaden-and-build theory of positive emotions. Philosophical Transactions of the Royal Society of London. Series B: Biological Sciences, 359(1449), 1367-1378

Helliwell, J. F., Layard, R., & Sachs, J. D. (2019). World Happiness Report 2019. Sustainable Development Solutions Network.

Hofmann, S. G., Sawyer, A. T., Witt, A. A., & Oh, D. (2010). The effect of mindfulness-based therapy on anxiety and depression: A meta-analytic review. Journal of consulting and clinical psychology, 78(2), 169

Huppert, F. A., Baylis, N., & Keverne, B. (2012). The science of well-being. Oxford University Press.

Le Doux, J. E. (2000). Emotion circuits in the brain. Annual Review of Neuroscience, 23(1), 155-184.

Lyubomirsky, S. (2008). The how of happiness: A scientific approach to getting the life you want. Penguin.

Lyubomirsky, S., King, L., & Diener, E. (2005). The benefits of frequent positive affect: Does happiness lead to success?. Psychological Bulletin, 131(6), 803-855.

Lyubomirsky, S., Sheldon, K. M., & Schkade, D. (2005). Pursuing happiness: The architecture of sustainable change. Review of General Psychology, 9(2), 111-131.

Lyubomirsky, S., & Layous, K. (2013). How do simple positive activities

Lyubomirsky, S. (2017). The myths of happiness: What should make you happy, but doesn't, what shouldn't make you happy, but does. John Wiley & Sons.

Kringelbach, M. L., & Berridge, K. C. (2012). The joy of hedonia. Science, 337(6096), 1099-1100.

Mak, W. W., Ng, I. S., & Wong, C. C. (2016). Resilience: Enhancing well-being through the positive cognitive triad. Journal of Counseling Psychology, 63(1), 50-60.

Maslow, A. H. (1943). A theory of human motivation. Psychological Review, 50(4), 370–396. https://doi.org/10.1037/h0054346

Mihály Csíkszentmihályi (2011) Fluir: una psicología de la felicidad. Editorial Kairós, S. A.; N.º 1 edición.

Pressman, S. D., Jenkins, B. N., Moskowitz, J. T., & Baum, A. (2013). Positive affect and health: What do we know and where next should we go?. Annual Review of Psychology, 65, 629-651

Rousseau, Jean-Jacques. Discurso sobre el origen y los fundamentos de la desigualdad entre los hombres. https://www.cervantesvirtual.com/obra-visor/discurso-sobre-el-origen-de-la-desigualdad-entre-los-hombres—0/html/ff008a4c-82b1-11df-acc7-002185ce6064_5.html[1]

Ryan, R. M., & Deci, E. L. (2000). Self-determination theory and the facilitation of intrinsic motivation, social development, and well

---

1. https://www.cervantesvirtual.com/obra-visor/discurso-sobre-el-origen-de-la-desigualdad-entre-los-hombres--0/html/ff008a4c-82b1-11df-acc7-002185ce6064_5.html

Seligman, Martin. Authentic Happiness: Using the New Positive Psychology to Realize Your Potential for Lasting Fulfillment.

Seligman, M. E. (2002). Authentic happiness: Using the new positive psychology to realize your potential for lasting fulfillment. Simon and Schuster.

Seligman, M. E. P., Steen, T. A., Park, N., & Peterson, C. (2005). Positive psychology progress: empirical validation of interventions. American Psychologist, 60(5), 410-421

Seligman, M. E. P. (2011). Flourish: A visionary new understanding of happiness and well-being. Free Press.

Sheldon, K. M., & Lyubomirsky, S. (2006). How to increase and sustain positive emotion: The effects of expressing gratitude and visualizing best possible selves. Journal of Positive Psychology, 1(2), 73-82.

Tov, W., & Diener, E. (2019). The well-being of nations: Linking together trust, cooperation, and democracy. Social Indicators Research, 141(1), 299-324.

Veenhoven, R. (2008). Healthy happiness: Effects of happiness on physical health and the consequences for preventive health care. Journal of Happiness Studies, 9(3), 449-469

Veenhoven, R. (2019). Happiness in nations: Subjective appreciation of life in 56 nations 1946-2018. Journal of Happiness Studies, 20(4), 1105-1139.

Also by Iraya Ahemón García

libros para colorear
60 Cubist Faces to Color
70 buhos para colorear
70 Owls to Color

Standalone
El egocentrismo y la política en la era Trump
LA FELICIDAD. ANÁLISIS DE UN DESEO
Las teorías conspiranoicas. Análisis y discusión
OVNIS. En la frontera de la de la verdad y el mito
Egocentrism and Politics in the Trump Era
Seeking Serenity. From Anxiety to Serenity
Happiness: An Analysis of a Desire